Active Monologues
That Directors Want to Hear

D0060947

Active Monologues
That Directors Want to Hear

New In The Moment Monologues
That Will Land You The Role

Paul D. Bawek

Bell Crandall Publishing

Your Home for Active Monologues

Monologue Writing Opportunity
See page 92 for details

See page 92 for details

Bell Crandall Publishing
925 Fenton Lane, Building 8
Lakeland, FL 33809-4039

Performance rights information can be found on page 91

Library of Congress Cataloging-in-Publication Data
Active Monologues That Directors Want To Hear / Paul D. Bawek.
ISBN-13: 978-0-9904980-0-1
ISBN-10: 099049800X
1. Monologue. 2. Acting—Auditions. 3. Theatre 4. American Drama—20th century

Layout: Penoaks Publishing, www.penoaks.com
Cover design: Bradley D. Bawek

For my mother,
who taught me to believe.

Contents

Active Monologues for Men

Preface

Active Monologues That Directors Want To Hear contains original monologues in which all of the performance pieces use active rather than passive form.

I carefully crafted each monologue so the characters express an immediate need to one invisible partner in the present moment. The book does not contain pieces that simply narrate past events to a general audience with long explanations of action. The monologues come alive in present-tense, in-the-moment language, the kind that casting directors in today's market place want to hear.

I write this book in response to what I consider a great need in the canon of monologue literature. As an actor and acting coach, I spent years searching plays and monologue books for active speeches. In time, I grew tired of looking for acceptable selections, and decided to write a book containing the active monologues for which actors and teachers are searching.

I hope writers can see the enormous benefit for collections of all active monologues and that we can satisfy the demand for such readily accessible material for auditions and class work.

Acknowledgments

No one writes a book of monologues without drawing inspiration from various sources. I would like to thank the people I've met all across our wondrous country and abroad. You have inspired many of the characters and situations the reader will encounter within the pages of this book. A special thanks goes to my instructors and the students I coached over the years. Each one of you taught me a valuable lesson. A very appreciative thanks goes to Roger "Buck" Busfield and Timothy Busfield for teaching me the craft of theatre and the elements of good story telling, and to my former agent, Jacqueline Schultz, for always believing in me as a creative artist.

I especially want to thank the students at Florida Southern College. I will be forever grateful to student director, Nicole Stewart, and the actors who brought the monologue characters to life, Jen Ackerman, Janelle Allen, Kari Baker, Jessica Barlow, Mary Bogo, Lacey Brown, Joie Bucalo, Chelsea Canestraro, Cathy Cherenfant, Nicole Chidnese, Ashley Cook, Colleen Doherty, John Esbenshade, Liza Ernst, Mister Fitzgerald, Joanna Galin, Kellianne Greene, Christopher Tebo Hardin, Joseph Hedrick, Sanjin Kico Kunovac, Daniel Hayes, Justin Vanden Heuvel, Allison Issac, Kaci Kohlhepp, Caroline Law, Ashley Lee, Ryan Marsico, Jodner Martin, Melanie McCullough, Jennifer Mears, Krista Miller, Victoria Miller, Angela Munoz, Brittan Overby, Jason Parker, Molly Patton, Joseph Pilka, Alex Pilka, Rebecca Schild, Haily Stuart, Jonathon Timpanelli, Brendan Troost, Brad West, and Cortney West. I would also like to thank Dr. Catherine Eskin for her assistance.

A heart felt thank you must be expressed to my godson Nicholas A. Bawek for his aid, Roxanna Martin, for sharing her creative insight, to my family and friends for their support, especially my mother, for her faith and unconditional love.

Finding the Right Monologue

As an actor in the business of theatre, a majority of your future work will rely on the monologue audition and your choice of material remains one of the most important decisions you will make. The following suggestions will serve you well in your hunt for active monologues that will land you the job.

- Choose monologues appropriate to your age and type, where the character embodies many of the personal qualities you possess. Always audition with a piece from a role you fit perfectly. It shows the auditor you understand your type and the business of your profession.

- Choose monologues within your range and ability. Honestly assess your current life experience and emotional availability, along with strengths and weaknesses for playing specific actions. Auditors want to see you living truthfully in the given circumstances and, to do so, you must connect to characters' thoughts, wants, and feelings on a visceral level.

- Choose active monologues where the character engages another person in the moment and has a great need to communicate what they want from them. Stay away from monologues that merely retell stories of past events and those addressed solely to the audience.

- Choose monologues with a solid beginning, middle, and end. Choose pieces, which allow the listener to grasp character relationships and the basic argument of the event early in the piece. Make sure the core of the monologue has a build and the character emotionally invests in the argument. Finally, ensure the piece has a strong button at the end: a strong physical or emotional expression that clearly defines your characters' present circumstances, emotional state, and aspirations.

- Choose monologues where the character speaks to only one person. There are exceptions to this rule, but having only one partner allows a character to focus energy more specifically when pursuing the objective. Communicating needs to multiple partners or to a general audience diffuses the character's energy and weakens the dramatic effect.

- Choose monologues of an appropriate length for the audition or ones you can easily edit. Auditioning within the specified time limit sends a message that you can follow directions and can work within time constraints. Note: auditors often know if they like you after ten seconds of your audition. This is not just a saying—it is a fact—so shorter is always better.

- Choose contrasting pieces if performing two monologues. Contrast does not always mean a classical and a modern piece however; it could mean playing the seductress and the wallflower from different plays or a monologue by both brothers in *True West*.

- Choose monologues that casting directors have not likely seen. New material catches their attention.

- Choose monologues that you love and have a passion to perform. A strong desire to share your message with the world will enhance every aspect of your rehearsal process and performance.

- Choose pieces that reflect how you want to be seen. Your choice of monologue tells the auditors a great deal about you as a person and an artist.

- Do not choose monologues auditors may find vulgar or offensive. This includes pieces with drug addicts, sexual abuse victims, or characters using profane language.

- Do not choose monologues with long intense moments of screaming or crying. Characters in monologues may explode for a moment or shed a few tears but they must never linger there. The struggle to maintain control always creates more drama than an actual eruption.

- Do not choose a monologue where your character speaks to someone on the phone. This type of monologue forces your character's energy into the phone, and makes it impossible for you to grab and hold an auditors attention.

- Do not choose comedic monologues that resemble standup routines. You must actively pursue an objective and the objective must connect to your monologue partner.

Finding the right active monologues for your present type and abilities is a life-long process that will continue to evolve as you develop as an artist and human being. Wherever you find yourself on the journey, the following monologues will certainly excite and challenge you as you continue your quest.

Pre-Rehearsal Exercises

Exercise 1.
Discovering your type

Typecasting is a reality in the industry. If you do not believe me, watch a movie, a television show, a commercial, or go to the theatre in New York. Rarely, will you see anyone cast in these media without the appropriate look for the part. Agents divide their stable of actors in terms of age and type, and casting directors always request pictures from agents in terms of type. Every audition notice specifies a type, EG: "Angel: a very short, sixties, hippie-throw-back type and the compassionate old guru for neighborhood kids." You can act the compassion but if you are not short and not older, you are not getting an audition. Type casting affects everyone, even the best-known actors, so we might as well accept it as a fact of the business and move toward an understanding of how we can best define and market our type.

The following exercises will help you discover your type. Do not limit yourself to just one, and search for the type you are today, not the type you wish you were. Take heart, there is a great demand for all types in our business.

Part One
Preparation: A pen and seven copies of the role types listed on page eight, one for each person responding in 1a and 1b, and one for your final summation in 1c.

a) Ask three people who know you very well to circle the role types that fit you, and indicate their top three type choices.

6

b) Ask three complete strangers to circle role types they perceive to fit you and indicate their top three choices.
c) Compile your answers and summarize your findings.

Part Two
Preparation: A pen and paper

a) Ask three people who know you very well (different from those you questioned in Part One) if you remind them of any characters from film/TV/plays/fiction and record their answers.
b) Repeat 2a with three complete strangers (different from those you questioned in Part One) and record their answers.
c) Compile the answers and summarize the findings.

Role Types

Wallflower • Ivy League • Leading Man • Intellectual • Dumb Jock • Outdoorsman • Psychopath • Blue Collar • Evil Bad Guy • Plumber • Wise Judge • Devious Wife • Playboy • Mafia Wife • Sixties Hippie • Teacher • Best Friend • Cocky Athlete • Warrior • Beach Bum • Rock-n-Roller • Stoner • Power Boss • Nice Neighbor • Drunk • City Slicker • Naughty Nurse • Sadist • Cheerleader • Class President • Rebel • Manipulator • Likable Looser • Biker • Over Needy • Girl Next-Door • Loser • Sex Symbol • Eccentric Artist • Pimp • Drug Dealer • Garbage Person • Star • Village Idiot • Manley Woman • Slob • Soccer Mom • Eighties Yuppie • Goth • Class Clown • Effeminate Man • Hero • Psychologist • Wall Street Exec • Guru • Perfectionist • Homeless Person • Waitress • Punk Rocker • Snobby Rich Kid • Scientist • Perfect Mom • Loud Mouth Jerk • Bad Cop • Cowboy/Girl • Nerd to Beautiful • Mediator • Weak Victim • Smug Millionaire • Secretary • Strong/Silent • Annoying Sibling • Red Neck • Country Folk • Nurturing Mother • Bartender • Leading Lady • Abusive Husband • Good Cop • Angelic Priest • Insecure Poor Kid • Good Guy • Car Mechanic • Slimy Salesperson • Seductress • Street Walker • Flamboyant Friend • Nerd/Geek • Sweet Sibling • Hardened Criminal • Mafia Man • Skate Boarder • Hardedge Detective • Perfect Dad • Troubled Teen • Brimstone Preacher

8

Exercise 2.
Choosing a type-appropriate active monologue

Utilize the information acquired from "Finding the Right Monologue for You," and "Discovering Your Type," to find three type-appropriate active monologues that excite you. Have five people who know you extremely well read the three monologues and, 1) choose the one piece that best suits who you are, and, 2) the one character they believe you are perfect to play at this time in your life. Tabulate the results, assess responses, and choose a monologue accordingly.

Active Monologues
For Women

Ascending Tor

BELINDA RAY, a free-spirited cashier at the local convenience store, convinces her ex-boyfriend that his advances are no longer desired.

BELINDA RAY: You love me? Am I supposed to call the paper now? Put in one of those corny want ads where there's a picture of us smiling like we were just hit over the head with a two by four? "Hey y'all, Dilbert loves Belinda."— Don't you ever say that to me. People in love do crazy things. People steal for love, and kill for love, and shave places they shouldn't—Then they buy things they can't afford, and expect sex all the time because they spray-painted something stupid on an I-10 overpass. I am not washing your dishes, listening to your NASCAR rantings, or holding you when you're old and drooling all over your AC/DC t-shirt. Wipe it from your mind Dilbert, 'cause it will be a cold day in Tallahassee before I tell anyone I love 'em. I love this okra, this slab of beef, and the fact that I'm not wearing a bra in this heat. That's about all I'm lovin', you understand? ... Is that spray paint on your hands?

Elutriating Pasts

COLLEEN, the respectful daughter who was all but forgotten by her biological father, explains why she has decided to shut him out of her life.

COLLEEN: I'm not a little girl, Dad. Buying me an expensive toy doesn't work any more. And I never really wanted the gifts anyway—I just wanted you to be there. You always made time for your new girlfriend and for Crystal—You made it to almost every one of her games, but when I played ... where were you? And I looked for you right up to the last one. I thought maybe this time. Maybe he'll finally be here. But ... *(Colleen breaks down. Slowly collecting herself as she speaks.)* To make me feel better Mom used to tell me it wasn't my fault. It was because I reminded you of her. I finally realized it wasn't her or me. It was you. You had a new life, and you were only taking what you wanted, and I wasn't a part of that. So I really can't accept this because I'm starting a new life. *(Starts to exit. Stops.)* Maybe ... it wasn't that you didn't have the time for me. Maybe you were just scared because you knew what I wanted, and you knew you didn't have it to give.

Vivendici

ERIN, a psychology major on a journey of self-actualization, enlightens her best friend to the benefits of expressing your true self.

ERIN: The only way to discover your own genius is to stop being what you think others want you to be, and just be you! Who cares if you fail? At least it will be you that fails. And who cares if people think you've gone completely woodpecker wacko? At least it will be you that is woodpecker wacko. I mean, look at me? You were born to be free Bondig. Born to be you. *(Singing a line from, "I Gotta Be Me," by Walter Marks.)* "I gotta be me, I've gotta be me!" Come on, when was the last time you felt an impulse to do something you wanted to do and just did it? I mean really— did it. I don't care what it was. *(Rips off her shirt and parades about as she sings her version of "Lady Marmalade.")* "Itchy, itchy, yeah, yeah, yeah, yeah. Itchy, itchy, shake your boot- tia. Café Mocha Latte, yeah, yeah. Come on let me know you're aliiiiiive!" Come on, do something you really want to do right now. No editing—just do it! *(Beat.)* That's the real you?

Mithridatism

LEE, a self-made businessperson who has made concessions in her life that leave her questioning her identity, finally confronts the man she loves with his racist world view.

LEE: You don't—*(Lee collects herself.)* I know you think of me as white—but I'm not white—and honey you can keep on trying to convince yourself we're not different and love changes everything, but when we leave this room you'll still be white and I'll still be "other." That's the bottom line. And it's not just the world outside this room that's prejudiced, it's you Frank—because as long as you only see me and accept me in your white perspective you'll never truly see me. So don't tell me you're not prejudiced until you're willing to put yourself in my shoes and see the world from my point of view. Don't tell me you're not prejudiced until you come out from around the illusion that we're all the same—because we are not the same. This is a white man's world, Frank, and I am not white. And you seeing me as such negates my entire existence. If you see me as white—I'm not here. I'm nothing to you. Because I'm not white Frank! I'm "other"! And I know you give money to charities to help the "other," and you love the "other," but you only do it so the "other"—including me—will rise above their circumstances to be more like you. White like you! And that, Frank, is the worst kind of racist, the one who doesn't even know he is.

15

671.69 Degrees

EVE, the class president, convinces a classmate that she will stand up for her in the future.

EVE: I was there when your car wouldn't start, and in the locker room—but I didn't think I could do anything. I wanted to—I did, and I should've—and in the hallway last week—I didn't want to deal with it, so I looked away—I knew what you must have been going through but I just let it happen, because I was afraid of what they would say—what they would think about me. It wasn't my problem—I didn't do it, so why should I worry about it. It wasn't my fault it was happening ... but it was ... because I could have done something—And I can't tell you how sorry I am for that. *(Beat. On the verge of tears.)* I want you to know that I'll be there for you next time. OK? I promise. I don't care what they say. I'll be there if you need me. ... I'm so sorry they did this to you ... I'm so sorry.

Overstocked

MOLLY, a stock person at a local Pharmacy who dreams of making it big in commercials, convinces a co-worker that her first audition was a huge success.

MOLLY: No, I don't care how I'm supposed to restock the suppositories because I'm standing here thinking, when is that phone going to ring? Maybe my battery is dead, maybe there's no signal—Don't, I've checked it fifteen times already. *(Laughs.)* And it is all because of the black cat that ran in front of my car today and the salt I spilled at Cinco de Mayo. I've been waiting for that one to catch up with me but why today? Why? I nailed the audition Shay. It was for the SPCA—or something like that—and I wrote this touchy feely animal thing. *(Preparing as if she were a method actor. Dead serious.)* "Have you seen my cow? Has anyone seen my cow? It's a Jersey cow. Oh my cow, my cow, my cow. Oh my cow, my cow, my Jersey cow. What ... will ... I ... do ... now? *(Leans head back and bellows in pain.)* Ahhhh! Hey stranger, have you seen my cow or my goat? Has anyone seen my goat? It's a Billy goat. It was walking near the moat. Oh my goat, my goat, my goat. Oh my goat, my goat, my Billy goat. My goat, my cow, what ... will ... I ... do...?" *(Sheds a fake tear and drops character.)* And scene. You should have seen them. At the end they were holding their breath just waiting for the ... "now?" They were so moved by my performance they couldn't say anything for like a minute. They just covered their mouths and started shaking—They couldn't even look at me they were so ... What? What's so funny?

No Other Love

BARTLET, an executive for a medical sales company, admonishes her younger brother for making everything a competition.

BARTLET: I'm not going to tell you. It's not a competition, Simon! It doesn't matter if I make more money than you! When are you going to grow up? And Mom does not treat my kids any different than yours. She is very careful to make sure they get the same things for their birthdays and Christmas, but you always find one little thing—"Well, that one's a better color than Andrea's." It's never good enough. Dad visited me more often because he liked my husband more than he liked your wife. It had nothing to do with you or me. You're all he talked about when he was here. "Simon is doing great." "Did you hear that Simon got the promotion?" "Simon's building a tree house like the one I built you kids." Don't look at me like that. You were always the favorite. The golden child, but you couldn't stop keeping track of who got what long enough to see it! Think of it this way, with my new raise, I'll be making about twelve thousand more than you a year, but the iPhone covers we got last Christmas—yours was a better color. So we're even—and don't argue with me because you know I'm always right. And I'm better at math—Not that I'm keeping track.

Pebble Beach

SARAH, an elementary education major, explains to her fiancée why she doesn't want to fight anymore.

SARAH: I'm sorry. I don't want to fight anymore. What's happening right now means absolutely nothing—No, please listen to me ... When my grandma passed away last month, all I could think about was that she once watched my great grandmother pass away, and my great grandmother had watched my great-great grandmother pass away, and that's been going on generation after generation for centuries—and it made me feel completely insignificant. In the grand scheme of things ... how can I really matter? How can any of us matter? And I realized that's why we hold onto—why I hold onto things—why I make everything so important. The world won't remember that we fought here today. The waves will continue to come in and go out; people around the world will continue to work, and sleep, and die—In the future this argument will mean nothing to us, so why can't we see that before we even start. All of this is nothing. *(Tearing up.)* I just want to love you, to share my life with you ... because you make me feel significant.

Veer

JILL, a DMV clerk and primary care giver for her handicapped sister, attempts to make her sister face the facts about a career in comedy.

JILL: Face it, Gloria—it's not that funny when women do physical comedy. That goes double for a woman in a wheel chair with two prosthetic legs—it's just not funny. And I'm sorry to tell you this but your hero, Lucille Ball, isn't funny to people anymore. And even if she was a bazillion years ago, she had something you don't—two legs to stand on. Listen, it's not a sin if you perform a pratfall and never get a laugh, because even if you make it seem obvious, people will never understand why anyone with two artificial legs—in their right mind—would do one in the first place. They are automatically going to think the fall was real, and to them, that is not funny. And when you take off your leg and pretend to paddle back to your chair, also, not funny. And when you pull off your other leg, the walrus thing, *(Mimes putting a prosthetic leg up to each side of her mouth)* that is just plain freaky. To you, it may be hilarious, but to them, it's an unusually weird event that's going to force them back into therapy! So please, put your legs back on, and let's go get a taco salad.

Impressions

AVARONA, an eccentric recording star and art collector, seduces a writer from a popular entertainment magazine

AVARONA: I know what you're thinking. She's as mad as they say. How could an empty canvas be worth anything? *(Admiring an empty canvas on the wall.)* But this one ... Think of your life as a series of impressions, and every day you take out a blank canvas and begin to paint what you see beneath the dance. The peaceful glow of a morning ... and stroke. The tone and line of rage on the freeway, stroke; the warm tint of a smile in a busy café; the texture of fear and desire in the eyes of a stranger; each image finding its way onto your canvas, and at the end of the day ... it takes shape. I'm simply fascinated by the stratums of a moment. A precious work. Do you see your imprint? Your hue? Your ... stroke? Of course, tomorrow it will be an entirely different masterpiece, but with the same title: "Today." Do you like it, or would you like to add another touch of color on my canvas?

Who Came Here Last

BLAIR, a high school dropout searching for a sense of belonging, describes herself at an audition for a television reality show.

BLAIR: To the camera or—You, OK. Sorry. *(Beat.)* Hi. My name is Blair Penny and ... what I want the most in my life right now is to laugh again. I love to laugh. I do. There is nothing better in the world. And sometimes I want to love. I need to love because there is so much love inside of me it feels as if it's going to explode and cover the entire universe—or at least my front porch area—if I allowed it to, if I could only allow it to—I hate myself for that. I hate it! And sometimes, sometimes I'm uncertain. Do I really want to be on your reality TV show with millions of people watching me? And not just that, but all of it, terrorism, and unemployment, and the price of garden gnomes—I love gnomes—have you seen the prices? It all just makes me want to roll up in a tiny ball deep inside myself and cry, so I cry. Because when it's all said and the credits are rolling, I care about the price of tea in China. I don't really know what the price is right now, but I care, deeply. I do. So, that's me. That's Blair Penny. Is this going to be on TV?

Cindertreller

ANASTASIA, a commoner who married into wealth, convinces a possible heiress to delay her interview with a panel of elitists who must find her worthy of the fortune.

ANASTASIA: My dear lady, would you graciously step over here for a moment? *(Changes voice to street dialect.)* Don't take this the wrong way, but it seems to me you took the trailer park trash out of the trailer park, moved it to the Hamptons, dressed it up in Gucci and Versace, but you forgot to throw away the trash. I don't care how much that dress cost you. They're not going to accept anyone smacking her gum like a dime store hooker and talking like an overly-aroused trucker at a strip club. I'm not a native here, but I know what they expect, and if you want to collect the inheritance, I suggest you allow me to tell them you suddenly felt under the weather. "An infectious disease you caught in the West Indies, and you shall contact them when better." In the meantime, get back in the limousine, go to your uncle's estate, and don't speak to anyone— don't even open your mouth until I can meet with you privately. You'll have to trust me on this. I'll have you playing the Gatsby in no time. Until then, hide! My driver is waiting to take you directly home—and not a word. To anyone. *(Switches to refined dialect.)* So sorry you're feeling under the weather. Ta, ta ... for now.

Hemihedral

JENNIFER, a temp worker in Chicago who recently acquired an acute awareness of her biological clock, annihilates her less than committal boyfriend.

JENNIFER: What do you want me to say now? I asked you if you wanted to stay the night, and you said, "Well, I'm already here." That really makes me feel like you want to be here, doesn't it? "Well, I am already here." And you didn't even ask me out tonight. I had to ask you out for my own birthday. My ex asked me out and you didn't. And don't even start in about him—I didn't say "yes," because I thought it might be nice to go out to dinner with the guy I'm dating! So happy birthday to me! And don't you dare tell me I am being over sensitive again or I'll scream. And I'm not just over reacting because you got me kitchen knives for my birthday. Which—may I say—are fortunately for you, out of my reach! So just go, mister—"Well, I am *already* here." Go home so you can call me later to apologize; go home so you can ask to come back and stay the night; go home so I can say: "No. Stay home. I mean—you're *already there!*"

90211

KAILEY, a popular party girl with a devilish mean streak, justifies her behavior toward an unpopular student.

KAILEY: He touched my hand when he passed me my assignment. He actually, physically touched me. Who knows what he would've done next. It's Mrs. Peck's fault with her, "Let's all come together in Panther pride" crap, like that is ever going to happen. The geeks think sports are neolithic, the tree huggers are out saving muskrats, and the stoners don't even know they're there. Not to mention the goth crowd, who are outside the game debating where they should stick the next safety pin—and the drama kids who are running around pretending to be fairies or whatever. If you guys think we are ever going to "come together," you need a double dose of a face it pill. The jocks hate the stoners, the stoners hate the jocks; the geeks hate everyone but Einstein, the goths hate everyone including themselves, the tree huggers love everybody, but everybody—including the muskrats—hates them, and we just leave the drama kids alone because they wear tights. And why is it important that we all get along anyway? Do you think I am going to associate with Tobias Turlington when I leave here? I'll be dropping down my hater blockers and pretending he doesn't exist. You obviously don't understand the pressure I live with, Mr. Dawkins. They can be losers because they are, but me—things are expected of me. He had to be taught a lesson. No one touches us unless they're one of us. That's the rule. So I cut off his finger, big deal. It's not like I called his mother "old mother Hubbard who went to the cupboard." Hello?

Relations

CAROL, an up and coming real estate agent, tells her devoted husband that she feels alone in the world.

CAROL: I'm tired of being alone ... I'm not talking about being by myself—It happens when I'm in the middle of my job Joe, or at a party, and I'm listening to what people are saying, and I'm responding to what they're saying, but no matter how hard I try to connect ... I can't. And I thought maybe all I had to do was find you. Find the person who sees things like I do—who feels the same way about things. It doesn't mean I don't love you. I've never loved anyone more in my life—but in the quiet of the night ... I'm still just a speck of nothing that happened to land on the bed next to you. And even you can't be in here with me. I've tried, but you're not there Joe. It's just me, and I'm—*(Beat. On the verge of tears.)* I'm tired of being alone.

Orchid Moon

ATALLA, a recent high school graduate who moved to Seattle because she always liked the Space Needle, lambastes a customer for his continual harassment.

ATALLA: For the umpteenth time, German is not my nationality. I am full-blooded Alabaman. I was born and raised there, and lived my entire life there until I moved out here. And yes, this is a German restaurant, but this isn't Germany. This is Washington. Do you think everyone that serves french fries is French? Or serves ham is New Hampshire-ian? I sometimes get lost in the sauce, but I know you don't have to be from Idaho to serve potatoes, from New England to serve clam chowder, or from Wisconsin to serve Old Milwaukee. Oh, I surprised you with that one didn't I? Well I have plenty where that came from, sweet heart. I may be from Alabama, but I know the quickest way to empty a tub. And the reason I didn't ask your nationality, is because with all the time you spend with your boot in your mouth, I can tell you must be Italian. Get that one, pasta boy? Good. Now, do you want spätzle or the new gluten-free egg noodles with your order?

H2 Tomorrow

ANNORA, a studious young woman explains that, in her opinion, her instructor's new book has no feasible explanation for man's inception.

ANNORA: I guess I'm an ignorant fool then. Because I read your book, but I didn't find a reasonable explanation for how non-living matter became living matter. How did it happen? Energy, time, and chance won't change it. You can zap the "swampy ooze" with energy for a ka-zillion years, but the chance that it will create life are zero to none. Scientists have never been able to create artificial life from matter and energy and chance. They've always had to add knowledge to the equation, so my question is, where did the knowledge come from a billion years ago? The laws governing the organization of matter today are the same as they were then. The natural laws of science haven't changed. If scientists can't create life from matter, plus energy, plus chance, today, why should we believe it could happen at biogenesis? It's not a logical conclusion! It takes a huge leap of faith. How can anyone make that leap? All I'm asking, is that you teach the facts and theories, and let us have open discussions about them. Because if we say anything that remotely questions the holier-than-thou theory of evolution in here, we're branded a religious freak or an idiot. And I'm not talking about religion. I'm talking about science! So, yes, by your standard, I'm one of those ignorant fools.

Uncovered Ground

TONI, the enthusiastic president and founder of "Women For Women," tries to inspire the one woman attending her rally outside the student union.

TONI: Don't go! This is important! I don't know where everyone is—but we can start this rally with just the two of us. Together, we can start a movement against the dehumanization of our gender. Are you with me? *(Prepares for her speech.)* First, WFW, Women for Women, is requesting that all women who join our ranks wear full cut briefs over their clothes. *(Pulls out a pair of grandma panties and puts them on.)* That's right, we are going to wear grandma panties proud for the entire world to see. We're going to make underwear our outerwear. Our shield of honor, until the whole world sees that we will no longer be sexual objects for men's desires. We are women. Hear us roar. This is what our grandmas wore. We are women. Hear us roar. This is what our grandmas wore! Can you envision ten thousand women in grandma panties marching to the Capitol? Neither can I, but at WFW, we have a dream. We have a dream! Oh, and if you get a chance, be sure to call and thank our sponsor, Cleavage Bar and Restaurant. They donated money for the grandma panties, so if you know anyone who doesn't have a pair, just have her show up here tomorrow at ten. *(The lone attendee exits.)* Hope to see you then ... She'll come. *(Pulling up her grandma panties.)* Oh yeah! She's coming.

Finish Line

HOPE, an event planner in Boston who lost her foot in the Boston Marathon bombing, informs her husband that his actions haven't helped her move forward.

HOPE: Bart ... You have to stop asking me to talk about it—it has to stop! I don't want to go out with your business associates—don't you think I know they want to ask me?—And I'd bring it up if I wanted to, but leave that to me. I'd almost forgot about it and then you have to—I don't want to deal with this every night. I ran a marathon—my foot was blown off, and now I limp like Dr. House and can't hover over a toilet when I pee! Can we have supper and allow me to forget it for one second? I'm doing the best I can with this... *(Struggling to hold back the tears.)* Just don't bring it up every time we go out like I'm a poster child. I don't want people's sympathy—it doesn't help me to move on. Treat me like normal. I'm the same person. *(Laughs.)* Minus a foot—And not being able to hover over that toilet seat tonight was horrible—it was wicked nasty—I'm sorry, I ... I don't even care about the limp. I just want to be able to hover again.

Mississippi Moon

ADARA, a resilient young woman who lives alone in a shack near the Mississippi River, confronts a man she caught breaking into her home.

ADARA: You know what you are mister man? You like a sneaky snake slithering in the grass. Like a night crawler on a hot night in July after a good rain, coming out of your hole and growing big and long to enjoy the moist steaming warmth of mother earth. But I flashed my light on you—caught you good so you can't ever go back in that hole now. 'Cause I'm going to stick that big ol' worm. Going to stick it through, up, and around, and plunge it down into that river for all those hungry fishes to fight over. And fish don't talk; they don't understand, only listen to one thing, what they want ... and they take it. Just like you, huh? Coming in here in the dark and wanting what you want, doing what you do. Just like a big ol' fish you are. Want to swallow me whole, but you didn't see my hook, did ya? You didn't figure on me havin' no net over that door to catch a big ol' fish like you. But now you the bait, see? Now you be the one waiting for the strike in the night. You the one who'll be dangling in the deep dark Mississippi.

Vagarities

WENDY, a cosmetology student, warns a classmate about on-line dating.

WENDY: His on-line description will say he's tall, dark, and handsome, weight proportionate, educated, and balances his life between working in the operating room and boating. But it will turn out he's four foot ten, has an orangish-bronze spray-on tan, and a face that only a blind mother could love if she didn't have hands. He'll be weight proportionate, or was when he dropped out of school in the second grade, and the operating room will be one of the rooms he mops during the graveyard shift at the hospital. Oh, and his boat, it'll be a four inch model of the S.S. Minnow with Gilligan and the Skipper, and if you really like boating, you're more than welcome to join him in his oversized tub for a three-hour tour. You'll have no idea what he means by that, and you won't want to stick around to find out. I'm just saying, if you haven't met this guy in person yet, don't! No one ever tells the truth on those on-line dating sites. He probably has a hunch back, likes wearing diapers, been married seven times—of which, the fist four didn't count because they were his sisters—and he thinks the word upscale is a fishing term. So, no, I don't think you should meet the guy no matter who he says he is ... *(Slyly.)* What dating site was that on?

Oligopsony

GOLDIE, a legal secretary who is struggling to maintain her Minnesota nice, confronts a senior partner for his continued disrespect.

GOLDIE: Oh well, I'm sorry I asked for one moment of your precious life to respond to what must seem to you an invasion of your all-important glorious mind. No—you need to hear this you pompous, egotistical—Ooo, you make me want to swear! What gives you the right to treat me to treat any of us like that? You. You give you the right because you think you are more intelligent than us. You have no time to pander to the ignorant—no time for the little things or the little people in life. Well, do I have a revelation for you! We are all little people in this big world, including you. And by most standards, you are the smallest one of all. You are the one lacking intellect, because you're unable to understand that it's the little things that matter most to us little people. Like having patience, compassion, and—dare I say—a little bit of love for your fellow man. Not even love—just respect. Respect for another human being is pretty high on our list. But in your honor, the next time you growl at me, I'll be happy to bark back, but I'm not fetching your slippers! *(Goldie looks behind her and back to the senior partner.)* I don't know who said those things to you, but I'll be sure they are punished sir. *(Scolding herself.)* Bad girl—naughty girl, *(She slaps the top of her hand)* naughty, naughty girl! *(Laughs uncomfortably.)* I'll go get those slippers now—papers, now, sir, papers.

Relume

BROOKE, a college student who is home for Christmas break, confronts her mother for mistreating her father.

BROOKE: You had no idea because you never took the time to really listen! ... I would be lucky to find a guy like dad. He doesn't lie, he doesn't cheat, he works his fingers to the bone to give you everything you want, and he doesn't ask for anything in return—but your love. Do you even care about his feelings anymore? 'Cause I'll sit here and watch him do something nice for you, and every time you'll find a reason to completely shut him down. So yeah, it hurts me to see him unhappy. To see you nagging him to death for every little thing he does. If you don't care anymore, then leave him. Divorce him, but don't treat him like crap in front of me. Can't you at least pretend you care about him when I'm around? ... I can't come home to this anymore—I won't come home to this. Tell Dad I love him, and I had to go back because—tell him whatever you want. *(Brooke starts to exit and stops.)* Mom ... Merry Christmas.

Climbing Everest

DERIVIA, an east coast literary agent, enlightens a brilliant but egotistical novelist of his future status in American literature.

DERIVIA: (Chuckles) Will your book be remembered for generations to come? Let me put it to you this way ... "No." Hypothetically, the novel makes the top ten list, the Pulitzer, maybe. It's good, very good. Minimum, your book makes the high school reading list for the next ten years before being replaced by the voice of a new era. The fact is, one hundred years from now, very few people are going to be reading any of your novels. I don't care how good they are. Who still reads "Black Like Me," or "Siddhartha?" Seminal works, for their time, but ask anyone under thirty and you have your answer. I'm not saying what you write isn't important—it is—but it will not be remembered for generations to come. If you were born in the Czech Republic, in Prague, where they have statues of poets and novelists, then you would one day be a statue on Petrin Hill: Jan Neruda, Karel Macha, and you. Your statue would be right beside theirs, reminding people of your work for centuries. But in America, we have Washington, Jefferson, and Grant. What I'm saying is, in the end, you're a footnote, at best. If you need more than that, move to Prague, marry yourself a young Czech girl, and get a new agent—because I'm doing everything I can!

Erosia

KATRINA, a wallflower with a multiple personality disorder, prepares to murder another boy of interest.

KATRINA: Maybe it was the way you started stuttering when you met her. Then again, maybe it was the drool coming out the side of your mouth the entire time she was in the room! What you don't understand is she did all that prancing around so she can smile that knowing little smile that says, "he may be here with you, but you know that I can have him any time I want." It's always been like that. I've never been able to compete with her. And you? I thought maybe you were different, but you gave it up to her for a flirtatious smile. You could have held out for so much more, soo, sooo much more. But now you're stuck with me. I'm sorry, are the handcuffs too tight? Don't worry. I won't make you suffer—long. *(Laughs.)* Tell me I'm beautiful. Tell me I'm the one you want, and maybe I'll forgive you. Tell me I'm the one you long for, tell me! ... Mean it! ... *Mean it!* ... I don't believe you.

Connubial Skies

DR. LORRAIN, a young pediatrician, overwhelms her husband with the reasons why she doesn't want a child.

DR. LORRAIN: Think about it and see what I come up with. We're talking about a child and you make it sound like we're debating the purchase of a new car. This issue was settled, Thomas—What about my career? I'm not—Are you willing to give up your practice for five years? Are you ready to live your life with the constant fear that something terrible will happen to them one day? Are you ready for feedings at one and four a.m., and diapers, and spitting up, and living with someone who will only eat hot dogs for an entire year? Not to mention our free time or vacations—You can't send a child off to a kennel. And the school system—and puberty, and then they're out all night, the yard's not mowed, and they drop out of medical school because they don't want to pay the man. They want to be an actor, an artist, doing bad community theatre and despising you for selling out to the system, while they live in the basement with their "friend" and seventeen illegitimate children who call me grandma! I'm not sure I want to wake up one morning wondering where my life went, and feel guilty because I'm no longer worrying that something terrible might happen to them ... But for now, I'll just think about it, and see what I come up with.

Bemini

TANESHA, an outspoken city girl preparing for her weekend mall experience, struggles with growing older.

TANESHA (TANNY): I can't do this Keisha. I'm not spiced today, baby. I woke up this morning, and I found a wrinkle—do you see that? I'm barely out of my teenage years, and I'm completely falling apart. Crest strips for my teeth, cucumbers for my eyes, Retin A for my face, blueberries and pomegranates three times a day, exercise, yoga, twelve hundred calories—and hair is growing on my lip, see!? So don't try to convince me I don't look any older. I have underarm hair that is growing overnight like a Chia Pet on steroids! It's like I'm dying right in front of my own eyes, and all my hopes and dreams are—I was supposed to be the next Tyra! Me! That was my job. But now my only hope is getting work with a traveling freak show as the bearded lady! *(Inhaling a large breath of positive energy.)* No, no, no, no—don't you listen to that, Tanny girl. You're still hot, baby. You still fresh-out-of-the-oven-hot no matter if you have a bushel of hair coming out of your nose or cornrows growing out of your ears. You still have the sizzle, kanizzle, manizzle without bacon fat drizzle! *(Beat.)* There. All better. What are you looking at?

Halcyon Wind

LAURETTE, a young mother dying of cancer, struggles to say goodbye to her baby.

LAURETTE: *(Looks at sleeping child across the room and then at the letter in her hand. Beat.)* Dear God, please don't let them be just words to him. Let him feel my heart and know how much I love him—how much he is a part of me ... how much I want for him—If he could only know how much I want to be here for him, what I would give to be the one who wipes away his tears and makes it all better, the one who holds him when he's scared and tucks him in at night— *(Fighting back the tears.)* But God has other plans for you and me. (Beat.) I will always be here looking over you, and I pray you'll feel me holding you every time you read this letter ... because I will never leave you ... and I will never stop loving you.

Leman's Call

ANGEL, an overly dramatic young lady who recently joined the drama club, persuades a friend that she will be a star despite what others may believe.

ANGEL: I'll show them who has the real talent at this school. I don't care what Mr. Olivier says. How can anyone named Olivier know anything about theatre anyway? I just need to be seen by someone who knows what real talent is—and that someone is John Robert Powers. After he sees my audition, I'll be a star. I can do comedy. Wax on. *(Angel makes a circular motion with her arm; sweeps her hand in front of her face a la "The Karate Kid" hand gesture and strikes a comedic pose. Angel continues performing gesture and pose using alternate hands.)* Drama. Wax off. *(Gesture. Pose.)* I can do love, *(Gesture. Pose)* hate, *(Gesture. Pose)* joy, *(Gesture. Pose)* fear, *(Gesture. Pose)* death, *(Gesture. Pose)* and sex, *(Gesture. Pose)* and fear and sex! *(Gesture. Double pose. Repeats gesture with new poses.)* Then we'll see who's laughing. And I won't be bitter. And I won't forget all the little people back here who were cast in the play but don't deserve to touch the earth I walk on! Wax on. *(Gesture. Pose.)* They'll see. They will all see. Are you sure I wasn't on the cast list? Maybe I should check it—to make sure.

One and the Same

VISHA, a stockbroker in Philadelphia, plans her retaliation for not receiving a bonus check that was promised to her.

VISHA: Oh, I have the time off. I already took the time off. I can't change that now, but I didn't get the bonus check Mario promised me this quarter, so there is no way I can take a vacation! So I was thinking, maybe I'll just set up camp in my office: pictures of the ocean on the wall, the beach on my screen saver, sounds of ocean waves on the CD, lying there under a heat lamp in a string bikini and sunglasses. "In Cancun this morning, Mario, and having some big time fun!" Slapping on sunscreen, people in the office passing, you taking pictures of me, little wading pool, floaties, a cabana boy in a Speedo fanning me, or going to the bathroom—passing customers in the lobby—"Don't mind me, just using the loo, oh, and afterwards, you're all invited to join us for an early happy hour on the beach in Jamaica." And then, with our Speedo clad cabana boy leading the way—carrying a boom box, and passing out Red Stripes—we start a conga-line with the customers and dance them through the meeting room during mid-day reports—"Woo-hoo! Join the line boys. Come on. 'Man up, man up,' right Mario? 'Man up!' This is what we call 'creative use of funds,' right Mario? 'Creative use of funds!' 'Get with the program boys.' Woooo-hooo!" The sick thing is, I'd probably get the promotion I've deserved for the past two years, because I showed my shiny little heinie—the male chauvinist maggot monkey.

41

Trailing Knots

CHRIS, an automobile insurance agent, responds to her boyfriend's unexpected rejection.

CHRIS: Oh, come off it, Phil. We both sell car insurance. It is always someone's fault. I don't care what state you live in, there is always someone at fault. So, is it my fault you're leaving? Is it? You just said it wasn't—So it must be your fault ... And I'm sitting here smashed to pieces, and you have a dent! And don't even begin to think that you can cover everything, because I'm talking about what's inside the car. I'm talking about emotional duress, broken bones, and blood on the pavement, and your three hundred thousand bodily injury protection won't cover it! You can add up your BIPD and rental reimbursement, but you'll still come far from the damages at this scene. In case you change your mind—that's policy number 0294880 dash 01. You know where I work. *(Pause.)* Look ... If you're not ready, I can back up, give you some space ... Give me some time to make sure I have enough coverage. If there is going to be an accident, I ... I—*(Crumbles.)* I'd handle things better with more coverage.

Cyrano's Calling

ROXANNE, a college girl who had a tumultuous relationship with her movie star mom, informs a reporter that her deceased mother deserves to be remembered for more than her movie credits.

ROXANNE: Listen, my mom wasn't perfect by any means. The world knows that, thanks to you guys. She was still working on her demons—she hadn't stopped working—but she was always far more concerned about what she could give to other people. And yeah, I sometimes hated her for that, because it wasn't always me. But I never stopped believing in her, and—despite everything you guys wrote—I never stopped loving her. And I wish one of you Hollywood idiots would report something about her with substance—instead of your soulless drivel. She's not just a movie credit. She was ... an amazing person *(Fighting back the tears)* who touched a lot of lives ... You can quote me on that. And feel free to throw in the "Hollywood idiots" and the "soulless drivel"—because that pretty much sums you up.

Felicific Nights

KACI, a member of the college soccer team, admonishes her roommate for being a worrywart.

KACI: If you say another word I may kill you—seriously. You are going to love Dr. Smith's class, you know you're getting financial aid next year, and how can you worry about something that's four years from now? You're driving me crazy, Penelope. Every minute of your life is a five-alarm fire. Do you ever have a day that you don't worry yourself to death about something? No, you don't. And you're driving yourself and every one around you crazy. What if you graduate with honors, get a job right away, and all of your dreams come true? Are you still going to be worrying? Yes, you probably will, but I've had it up to here with all of it, and I'm not going to put up with it anymore! So from now on, when I come in, if you don't have something positive to say, don't say anything. And if you're worried about something, call someone who cares, because I don't. So just zip it shut, OK! ... Let's try this again, shall we? Hey Penelope, we won our game and I scored the winning goal! How was your day? ... I don't know who peed on your pop tart, but you need some serious help. You know that?

Vicissitudes

MARY, a massage therapist, whose boyfriend has transient global amnesia, tries to awaken him to their past relationship.

MARY: It's called transient global amnesia—You don't remember things, honey. But we've been here before, standing right here, and not in some déjà vu kind of way. Stop and think about it. Look at me. You have been here, looking into these eyes, and the question I asked was, "What could I ever give to you, Mr. Craig Cooper, that you don't already have?" And do you remember your answer? Do you remember? ... "Little ol' you, Mary, little ol' you." Remember? It's little ol' Mary. I'm right here—Look at me! I'm not going away until you understand who I am! Look at me. I know you're scared. I know you're unsure of who you are, and why you're here. But don't worry about that now. Just look into my eyes and think about what you see there. *(Beat. Mary breaks down.)* It's me baby. It's me ...

Machinul

IRINA, forced to work in a factory since childhood, attempts to remember what it was like outside the place where she's been held captive.

IRINA: It is difficult when you don't remember, Alverdo. I think I have dreams, but something must come in the night and steal them away from me ... What I wouldn't give to remember a dream—for one day of sunshine, a day outside these walls. Do you think it is day now? The sun must still rise. The sun ... "This is no place for us"—Do you remember? We said that. "The rich are spending a month in the country killing time that we can only hope for"—remember? But us, every day we are here, like machines, touching steel, making death. No dreams in the day and no dreams in the night ... I want to remember. I need to remember. (*Fights to hold back her tears.*) When was the last time you saw a flower, Alverdo? A flower. Do you remember what they looked like? We are still young. We should remember, but all we know is a thirst for what we have forgotten, and soon ... even our thirst will be gone.

Pyrolyze

ROSA, a cannery worker, admonishes a male co-worker for disrespecting her as a woman and a human being.

ROSA: My problem is men like you, Victor. You're always staring, always digging into our flesh. We can shut you down and walk away, get in our cars and drive away, but we can still feel you, like wolves, gnawing away at us. I've been telling you to stop since I came in here—but you don't care. When I leave, that feeling that filth will remain, but you don't care. Look at me! I am a human being with a mind, and a heart, and a soul, and you have no right to treat me like a piece of meat! ... Know, that when your daughter is born, your sins will be repaid on her. Everyday, men's eyes will consume her innocence. Everyday, their eyes will tear at her flesh and eat her alive till she is nothing but an empty shell. I will pray to Mary for her soul, and I'll pray for you—That you are struck blind the moment she is born, so you cannot see the animals devouring her ... *(Smiles.)* Have a blessed day, Victor DeJesus.

Microseisms

SANDY, a young lady trying to gain acceptance into the in-crowd, rebukes her mother for not acting her age.

SANDY: Girls in tube tops get in free? Where did you pull that one from, Mom? That's the funniest thing I've ever heard—Not! I can't believe you said that. And you were flirting with Zach and Tyler—Yes, you were! It was totally embarrassing. I'll never be able to look at them again without feeling like a complete loser-head. You knew I liked Zach, and now he's going to think that when I grow old, I'll look like that. Did you even look in the mirror before you came out here? You're totally a tube top drooper. We make fun of women like you at the mall—I can't believe this. You completely ruined everything. I'll never be able to show my face at school again. I might as well kill myself now because my life is over. Girls in tube tops get in free?! You're not a girl anymore, Mom, so just deal with it! ... Give me the tube top. Come on—Because I'm going to wear it—'cause the only way for them to forget *those*, is to see *these* in it, OK? I can catch them at the park and do damage control—I'll also need the car keys and cash. *(Holds out her hand.)* Come on. I'm not getting any younger here.

Hightus

SALLY, a well-intentioned but misguided young lady, convinces a fellow inmate why she isn't afraid of facing the authorities.

SALLY: At this very moment—underneath my dress—I'm wearing men's underwear ... On the outside you see this, but on the inside is one pair of tidy whities. And when I walk in front of that parole board and feel this one hundred percent cotton brushing up against my skin, there's no holding me back. And don't ask me why I tried it, or why it works, because some things are better left unexplained. Kinda like my love of fat men with one eye. I can't get enough of them fat one-eyed men. *(Singing her version of Streisand's "My Man.")* "Oh, fat men, I love them so, they'll never know." And don't ask me why I tried that neither, because I know that is better left unexplained ... So, nope, I'm not afraid. When I go in there, I'll look them right in the eyes, and this time they'll believe me. They'll have to believe me. The mayor's kids locked me in the cellar long before they started the house on fire. And Andy, the deputy in Hightus—who is fat, I mean fat-fat—well, he believes me. Good ol' Andy. He doesn't have one eye, but I'm thinking if I ask him real nice, he'll take one out for me. That's my dream anyway. Can't help but dream real big when you live in Hightus.

Adventive a Go-Go

DIAMOND, a dancer at the Go-Go Club, inadvertently takes out the pain of her past on an unsuspecting customer.

DIAMOND: *(Dancing seductively in front of her client.)* Uh, huh. Yes sir, I could tell straight off you weren't like the others here, honey. You're so handsome. I bet your two little daughters are as cute as their daddy, mmm? ... Now you listen to me if you want to keep what's yours. You better tell those girls they are smart and pretty—no matter if they're dumb as rocks and plain as shredded wheat. And you better tell them that you love'em over and over again, and when you think you've told them enough, tell'em ten thousand times more! 'Cause a little girl needs to know her daddy loves her no matter what, and that she's beautiful—even if she has a skinned-up knee, and one tooth showin', you understand?! A daddy's love can make all the pain go away, but if he don't tell—then he don't care, and if he don't care, then you ain't nothin'. You ain't nothin', understand? Like it would be better if you was dead. Then that's it. You dead. And you doin' everything you can to kill yourself 'cause you not livin' anyway. Some do it fast and some do it slows, but we all dead. We all dead because of our daddies, you understand? *(Beat.)* That will be one hundred dollars, sweetheart.

Planoblast

BETH, an upper class shoe fanatic, tells her husband why it is so difficult to throw away her old shoes.

BETH: Can't we build a bigger closet? ... Jacob, I can't just throw them away. They're my shoes. You don't understand. Some people have pictures to remember things. I have my shoes. Every day I walk in the closet I see the Sierra Nevada's, I see Copenhagen, I see Vienna. What will I have left? *(List your city and State.)* I am more than that. I am the cobble stone streets of Rome; I am the Mayan ruins of the Yucatan Peninsula; *(Points to her feet)* I am the pain I feel right now. Shall I throw them out as well? *(Pulling shoes off)* Because it will do me no good to have a reminder of today. Go ahead and take them. Take away our first kiss; take away the first time you told me you loved me; take away the night with you in the pink g-string and pasties. Take them. *(Holds out the pair of shoes in her hand.)* And take these as well, because I can't live in a house with this memory. *Take them!* *(Hugs the pair of shoes.)* All I ask is that you make it somewhere close so I can visit.

Active Monologues
For Men

Changes

PAUL, a New York architect and former self-proclaimed bachelor, argues with his fiancée about an answer on a pre-marriage counseling questionnaire.

PAUL: Let me get this straight. You asked me, if you and I and my friends and my mother were all on a ship that was sinking and I could only save one of you, who would I save? And I said, I'd save my mother—and that's the wrong answer? How can that be the wrong answer? You can swim. My mother can't swim. She can't even dog paddle. And they wonder why people don't get married in the Catholic church anymore. That's a pretty good reason. You'd leave there seeing the dead bodies of your family and friends floating around you. Bye Jimmy, Vince, Ma. Sorry I can't save you, but I'm married now. But don't worry Mom, she's a lot like you. OK, I didn't mean that. I know you are nothing like my mother, and at times you can't even stand to be around her, but the poor woman is dead for Pete's sake. She's bloated and decaying on the bottom of the ocean floor! But to answer your question—now that I fully understand the implications of the question—I would save you. Even if my mother were screaming my name at the top of her old, tired, and soon to be decaying lungs, I would save you. Are you happy now?

Disinter

WASHINGTON, an African American man who was recently promoted into upper management, tells a blatantly racist regional manager his perception of what it is like to live as a black American.

WASHINGTON: You honestly think I can speak for all black people? Can you speak for all "your people?" And what do white folks think about that, Dell? *(As Dell.)* "You know, on behalf of all white people, I think I can safely say we all prefer cantaloupe." Really? Well, I don't feel qualified to speak for all my people. I know that when we go shopping, we'll be fortunate to find more than one doll, one magazine, or one greeting card created specifically for us. That, I know. And when we shop, we know the eyes of every security guard in the store will be on us. And if we ask to see the person in charge, they probably won't be one of us. And we know it will be more difficult for us to find work, and when we do, others won't think it was because of our qualifications, it will be because we are one of "those people," and if—heaven forbid—we are ever late for anything at that job, it'll be because we are one of "those people." And when "those people" leave work, they can expect people to cross the street to avoid them, expect to be pulled over and harassed by the police, and expect that one or more of their white neighbors will be pissed off because some of "those people" moved in next door. I think I can safely say that a large percentage of my people deal with these issues every day, but what they think about it, I just don't know, Dell. What do all "your people" think about it?

Ascending Tor

TINY, a know-it-all truck driver informs an old truck driving buddy how to save the planet from global warming.

TINY: If they want to fix this thing, Al Gore and all his global warming buddies need to start talking about cow farts. 'Cause methane is twenty three times more potent than C02 at trapping heat—twenty three times! You ever let a good one go when you're driving? It's like setting your butt cheeks on fire with a Bunsen burner. And cows emit more methane in a day than all of the trains, planes, and automobiles in the entire world. That means that one-day of cow farts equals twenty-three days of driving for all the world's transportation vehicles combined. The whole world can drive for an entire year, and cows will do the same damage to the ozone layer in fifteen and a half days. That's twenty-three years of fart damage for every year of driving. Do the math. We don't have to sell our trucks to save the planet. We need to kill cows. I know they ain't going to like that in India—but it's that simple. All I have to say is big Al better figure out how to make cows fart less before he thinks about coming after me for my carbon footprint. "Kill a cow and save the planet." That's what people should be talking about. You want to save the earth for your kids? Eat a steak ... If the government is serious about this, they need to start up a cash for cows deal like they did for our trucks. Only this time, you turn in a cow, and you get your truck back.

By Design

MARK, a young schoolteacher visiting his dying mother at the hospital, reveals the reason why he can't let go.

MARK: They're going to pull the plug Mom ... I've been holding them off, but there's not a lot I can do. *(Beat.)* Listen, the gum under the pew—that was me. And I was the one who took the car that night. And the wine ... technically, it wasn't a miracle that it turned into water. It was a miracle I didn't toss my cookies all over Marsha Fitzberry, but I don't think God had anything to do with that. *(Beat.)* You remember when I was little, and you'd sit with me when I'd say my prayers? And every night you'd kiss me on the forehead and tell me to sleep tight because God would keep me in his arms till the morning? You remember that? ... Well, I never told you this, but after you turned out the light, I'd always say one more prayer. I'd look up to God, and tell him how much I loved you, and I'd ask him to take me before he ever took you because, I—I couldn't imagine living without my mommy. *(Struggling to fight back the tears.)* The truth is ... I still can't imagine it, Mom ... I can't.

Generating Addis

ADDIS, a highly-strung horticulture major, explains why he is afraid of his girlfriend meeting his parents.

ADDIS: I'm not saying "don't go." I'm saying, if you have anything else you want to do ... No, I'm not afraid of my parents meeting you. I'm afraid of you meeting my parents. I love them and everything—OK—I'm lying—If I met my parents and they weren't my parents, I wouldn't like them. They wouldn't be my friends—enemies, maybe. In high school they were the un-cool parents, and now they're the hypocritical, politically incorrect people Jon Stewart makes fun of, and you'll see them and see me in twenty years, and suddenly I'm playing Bocce Ball and everything I own is polyester—which I know is coming back—but—I'll never see you again! You'll say it won't matter, but they make a very big impression. And then one day, you'll say I'm like my father, and I'll freak, and whack quack it's over. I can't believe I just said whack quack—It's starting already! Who in their right mind would say, whack quack! What does it mean? Whack quack what? You knocked off a duck? It makes no sense! You see my point? I'm not saying don't go—I'm saying ... don't go. Do you see the difference?

107 Stories

CARTER, a fire fighter, convinces a friend that nothing will erase the memories of Sept. 11, 2001.

CARTER: It can be a peaceful morning, my kids will yell something from the street, and I'm back there—like that. *(Snaps his fingers.)* It can be something about the food I'm eating, or a smell, or ... It's a part-a who I am now. I lost a lot of brothers that day, a lot of family—a guy doesn't... *(Fights back the tears. Beat.)* I don't care how many flags they wave or songs they sing out there. Bin Laden's death won't change it. I thank God I have the capacity to forgive, but I wish He would let me forget ... I saw this little Jewish man and an Arab Muslim helping an older gentleman out of an office on the 86th floor. The three of them made it out together. When things get hard, I think about that. God is in a moment like that. It doesn't make it all right, but it helps. Those kids out there don't know anything. This guy was a scary little monster under their bed, but it was real for the people inside the towers. I don't care how many terrorists they kill, or monuments they build—it doesn't go away. You take it to the grave, a thing like that ... You take it to the grave.

Slated

LAZARUS, a young man who has been missing from a school for the blind for several months, tells a forest ranger why he desires to be left alone in the Adirondacks.

LAZARUS: Have you ever felt the air awakened by the touch of the sun or listened to the trees sing, and knew you were where you were meant to be? ... I'm lost in the city. It confuses me. But here, there is a rhythm I can understand. She speaks and I hear her. She dances and I feel her. For the first time in my life, I'm fully alive ... You have a gift, a gift of sight. You can see me, but what do you see? Do you see someone in the middle of nowhere who is blind, and lost, and in need of help? If that's the case, close your eyes and listen. It's the only way you'll understand I'm not lost here. I'm not alone. Close them. Close them and listen. Listen like you've never heard before. Listen. *(Beat. On the verge of tears.)* Twenty-seven steps to the stream, listen ... mulberries to the north at the second incline, burdock root on the east slope, stinging nettles all along this hillside, and the trees telling you everything you need to know. Can you see it? ... If anyone asks ... you don't have to lie. Tell them you didn't find anyone that was lost ... please.

Primary Engagement

LARRY, a very fast-talking paranoid schizophrenic, overwhelms his blind date with his fear of being detected by Big Brother.

LARRY: Yeah, it was nice of Marsha to set us up like this, but I can't come in because you're watching television. If Big Brother sees I'm here, that will be it. They'll place an agent with a chip laser on the roof and next time I'm here, bang! I'm under their control. If it hears my voice for more than three point eight five one thousandth of a second it will identify me. They send you messages through it, you know. "War is good." "Love Big Brother." "Goat. It's what's for dinner." The last one changes depending on who is funding the subliminercials. I called for a pizza two years ago, and the lady asks if I was sure I wanted extra cheese and would I be paying with cash—because my record showed I had high cholesterol, my credit card was close to maxing out, and she wanted to make sure I'd still fit in the shorts I just bought for my vacation to Vegas. That was the day I threw away my credit cards, bankcards, and any electronic device I had. *(He pulls out a pair of reading glasses with a fake nose attached.)* I got these before they hid GPS systems in everything. I know this is a first date, but could you do me a favor and not call me by my name. They can read your lips on those cameras on street signals. Just call me *(He changes his body shape and voice)* John Michael Washington Gonzales Lincoln Summerfield Smith—the third. You ready to go?

Ivy Society

BOSTON, a waiter, begs his female friend to stay the night in order to protect him from a man he thinks is in love with him.

BOSTON: You have to stay, Judy. He doesn't own a car, and I know he's going to ask to stay here after the party—and I don't want to be left alone with him. The guy wears lime, and he calls me before noon on a Saturday to tell me about clothing sales. You see what I'm saying. Today, after work, he tried to get under my umbrella. Men don't do that. It's an unspoken rule—you just don't do that. And the fact that he remembered my birthday last week is off the chart wrong. Guys don't remember other guys' birthdays. If we do, we pretend we didn't, and we definitely don't buy each other presents unless our girlfriend forces us to—and it's never underwear. That I know is a major guy rule. It's written in an ancient text somewhere. It's like the eleventh commandment or something. "Thou shall not buy or have knowledge of another man's undies." You don't want to know what they were, believe me. *(Chortling.)* You want to know the real kicker? ... He once told me my fly was down. Need I say more?

Lavatation

CORBIN, a recluse living on the outskirts of town, informs sergeant Kline why he crucified five Catholic schoolgirls.

CORBIN: Did I touch'em? *(Beat.)* What do you think, Sergeant? ... What happens when you see a pretty young girl with all the innocence you lost so long ago? Are you wantin' to suck it right out of her? To show her the lust and filth of yer mind? ... How do you protect her then? The world's full of darkness, and sooner or later the devil will rise and steal them away like he did you. You gotta keep the little ones pure. Keep'em pure like when you were just a boy. Do you remember that? Being pure? ... I didn't *touch'em*—not any of 'em! You don't do nothin' but for a last prayer before ya nail her pure little hands and feet to the cross. A cross you made with your own sweat and blood, a cross that will send her to heaven innocent. Like angels they are. Sendin' God an angel—Ya can't *touch'em*, you understand?! They'd be like you! ... They'd be no better than you.

Struthious Flight

MAXIMILLION MANNERS, an activist who spends his life protesting the injustices of the world, searches frantically for a cause to feed his growing ego.

MAXIMILLION: I need a fix and I need it soon, Koko. The adrenaline is already wearing off from eating all those monkeys in a barrel to protest the treatment of gorillas in captivity. They're just not lasting like they used to. When I ate that Boeing 747 wing protesting the removal of hard-earned frequent flyer miles, the euphoria lasted a good year, or swallowing all those dead clown noses for hard working street mimes. Those were feasts I tell you! They brought awareness to the plight of those whose voices were not being heard—who could not speak for themselves. I was their mouthpiece. I was their savior. And to quench my desire, I need it again, Koko. I need a cause and I need it big. Bigger than Elvis ... Wait a second. It's coming to me ... I'm seeing an outfit so glorious it would raise Liberace from the dead, my hips gyrating to hunk of "Burning Love," and me, eating the iron gates of Graceland to stop the woes and wailings of the poverty-stricken men and women who die daily in the rhinestone mines across the world! Are you with me, Koko? Are you with me? ... What do you mean—most of them are man-made?

Defenestrating Henry

JAYME, a college senior who has reason to believe his fiancée may have cheated on him, struggles to save the relationship.

JAYME: You didn't listen to what I said! No—you're not—Will you shut up for one second and *listen*!? *Please!* *(Beat.)* Thank you ... You think I came over here to upset you? Stoje, you are the air I breathe. I wake up in the morning and think about what I can do to make your day better. I don't think it's out of line for me to ask a simple question, and that's all it was, a simple question. "Is this Ken's coat?" That's all I said. Was I thinking you had him over last night and screwed him? No. I was thinking maybe he stopped over to say his last goodbye before the wedding; you had a nice talk, and he happened to forget his coat. And right now, I need you to tell me that's what happened because we can't start our lives together with me knowing anything different. And the hell with truth and honesty, because sometimes it's just better to lie. So don't accuse me of accusing you of anything, and don't tell me you were with Ken last night. Don't tell me anything but that you love-me-enough, that when I come back here, you will greet me as if nothing has happened. And you will do it because I am the air you breathe, and you can't imagine a life without me. *(Beat. Breaks down. Pulling himself together.)* I'll see you in an hour or so—and ... It would be nice if the coat were gone.

Pebbles Dropping

BILL, a guardian angel disguised as a deliveryman, convinces a young lady that her life on earth is important.

BILL: We've all experienced uncertainty ... Everyone has moments of doubt, Sarah. We think we're the only ones, and no one else could ever understand. But the truth is, a lot of people on this earth are just like you ... Look at the tips of your fingers. Just look. Do you see all those lines? Do you see how the pattern starts in the middle of each finger and circles out? Like someone dropped a little pebble in the water and it rippled outwards, each line affecting the shape of the next line, each line dictating where the next line must logically go. I think the patterns on our fingers mirror life. The pebble drops when we come in contact with another human being, and the affect of that meeting is the wave rippling out. Each meeting affecting the shape of our next wave, each wave—in a small, but significant way—dictating where the next one will go. But we have to be there for the meeting to happen—for the pebble to drop—because if we're not, a billion other waves are affected. I don't think people realize the influence their existence has on others. I don't think we comprehend how a simple smile, a pleasant "hello," or the smallest act of kindness can start a wave that could change the world as we know it. Every day—every second—a pebble drops, and the waves begin. It's a simple choice, Sarah. The question is, which one are you going to make?

Homeland

STEVE, an overly competitive ex-jock, convinces a friend to help him get revenge on a nemesis from his past.

STEVE: You have to help me on this one—that is, her. That's the girl who broke my mamma's back ... You know the game where you walk down the sidewalk and try to distract the other kid—so they'll step on a crack—and when they do, they break their mother's back? Well, that's her. She's the one who broke my mamma's back. And I was the king of the walk. The king of step-on-a-crack-and-break-your-momma's-back, the king of all of San Francisco. Young children whispered when I passed, "There he is, the king of crack. No one ever broke his mamma's back." No, not my mama. For hundreds—thousands—of matches I was undefeated, the undisputed champion, and then she came along—And there wasn't a moment that she let me forget it—with her knowing little smiles and smirks. Look at her. She's still smirking ... All right, all you have to do is send her a drink and make a totally inappropriate move on her. Then, I'll come to the rescue, take her outside for an innocent stroll and crack! I'll be back. No, I'm not kidding.

First Kiss

BOBBY, a sweet and excitable schoolboy, attempts to navigate the uncertain waters leading to the wondrous moment of a first kiss.

BOBBY: I'll tell you if you tell me. I'll even tell you if you don't tell me because I've been wanting to tell you for awhile—sorry, I'll slow down. It's just, I—I—I like you, Krissy, and I've been wanting to—well, wanting to—kiss you goodnight for—well, awhile now, and it's all that I ever think about, you know. I wake up in the morning and I think about it, and then I think about it all day at school, and I don't know what to do because—well, I didn't want to kiss you if you didn't want me to. 'Cause the first kiss has to be right. It has to be at the perfect moment, with the right mood, and the right person. Like the movies, they don't talk about it, it just kind of happens, like magic—and I just talked about it— not that you wanted to, I'm not saying—You do? ... You don't suppose you could forget I talked about it, because I don't even remember what I was talking about. Was I talking about something? I don't even remember—yes, I'll be quiet now. *(Pause.)* The moon sure is nice.

Meridians

AaTMICK, an inner city acting instructor who is frustrated with his inability to reach his students, tries to convince a young man of promise to share himself with the audience.

AaTMICK: I said get out! Is that too difficult to understand? ... What? You want me to praise you for your brilliant performance tonight? You knew your lines, so bravo! *(Mockingly applauds Perez.)* But don't fool yourself, Perez, you're like all the rest of them. You act tough and bitch about how horrible your life is, but you don't do a damn thing to change it. You want to be an actor? Then have the balls to tear away your flesh piece by piece, reach inside, rip out your heart, and feed it to the audience. That's what they want in the real world. That's what they come for. You want to be good? Then be ready to feed them with your life. I don't care who hurt you, and I don't care what they did. You only lose if you keep thinking they took anything away from you. It's still there, Perez, stronger than it ever was. It just can't find its way through the mack-daddy act you put on— and all your excuses ... get out. Now! Before I tell you what I really think.

Carthage

ROBERT, a man who recently lost his job and is losing his family, attempts to tell his four-year-old daughter that he is moving out of their home.

ROBERT: Suzie? Susan. Sue Bear. Will you put down the damn doll and *listen to me*! I'm sorry. No, it's Ok. Daddy didn't mean to yell at you. He didn't and he's sorry. It's just that daddy is a little bit on edge right now and—well ... You know when you're playing dolls, and you love that doll so much because it means the world to you—it is the world to you—and then someone takes your doll, so you get upset, and you scream, "Give me my doll back! Give it back! *I want my dolly*"—And you don't know what to do because whoever took it refuses to let you back in. And you thought you were working it out. You thought you were correcting things and then bang! It's all gone. And all your plans, they just—and you miss them so much—and they're right there—and you feel there must be some way, and daddy—he's losing his doll, see—and he doesn't know what to say because he loves her so much that he can't imagine a world without that smiling face looking up at him every morning, and her tired little arms around his neck when he carries her to bed, and—and ... *(Struggling to fight back the tears.)* I'm sorry. I'm so sorry. Daddy didn't mean to yell.

Willesden Lane

CARVER, a veterinarian who has all but given up on love, overwhelms his female friend with the reasons why he would never want to be a woman.

CARVER: I can think like a woman, Leigh. That's the reason I would never want to be one. Sorry, but why would I want to live my entire life knowing I would never meet a man who had everything I wanted? Ever. Right now, there are thousands of women out there searching for their ideal husband, the über-man out of a romance novel, but he doesn't exist. And I think, way down deep, they know it. They know it's a fallacy, a fairytale, but they keep searching. They're like those ladies who stand in their front yards calling their cats in for dinner. It doesn't work. The cat's not coming. It's a cat. It's not a dog. And it will never be a dog. And there's something very sad about that, very sad. Men, on the other hand, can have everything they want in a woman because we are very simple creatures. We either like you the way you are and want to sleep with you for the rest of our lives, or we don't. It's that simple. There's no mystery to it. To us, it is what it is. That's why we don't go outside and call our cats in for dinner. They're cats!

Six Doors and a Lady

PETER, a regional bank manager, tells a neighbor how he feels about sucking up to his boss.

PETER: "A good day?" I missed the train! And you know what that means, don't you? It means I'll have to deal with their snivels, and sneers, and "late again, are we?" And I'm only going to gain points with Mr. Hornsby. What I'd like to do—I'd like to call them up and say, "I missed the morning train, so I've decided not to come up this weekend because— the truth is—I really don't like you. To be perfectly honest, I don't even like Mr. Hornsby. In fact, I despise him and the whole lot of you posh poshing this and that's, and "Little Caroline is going to Cambridge next year, and you must come and visit us on the Cape." They know very well that I know they don't want me there, any more than I want to be there. "No, sorry. The truth is, Mr. Hornsby, I'd rather be home baking muffins. In fact, I'd rather walk through fire, put a long needle in my eye, and a jack hammer up my"—*I can't believe I missed the damn train!* But don't get me wrong. Life is good. Can't complain, absolutely wonderful!

The Nucleus

KELTON, a Vietnam veteran, tells his son why he refuses to allow him to enlist in the military.

KELTON: Sit down. I said *sit down! (Beat.)* I want you to imagine sitting in a classroom at your high school with all your best friends, your best buds, and you're given the order to stay in your seats no matter what happens—no matter what. And one second you're looking at them, and it's completely silent, and the next second, their arms and legs are being blown off all around you. Blood is spitting everywhere, and they're screaming for help, and you have to sit there in the blood and the guts till you can't take it anymore, and you snap, and you run. You run outside the classroom shooting and screaming because you want to be dead. You want to die—so it will be over—but as long as you're still breathing, it's never over, never ... If you want to enlist, pick up the gun and put a hole right here *(Points to his heart)*, because that's the only way the nightmare is going to end for me. And that's the only way you're going, over my dead body. *(Pause.)* Now, where'd you hide my damn bottle?

Dawn in Nevada

MR. DAVE, the ghost of famous theatre director and acting coach David Belasco convinces an unemployed showgirl to train with him.

MR. DAVE: A dancer in Las Vegas? Burlesque I assume—but a dancer none-the-less. Yes, a dancer, a most noble and admirable profession. And I am sure you are—were—very good at what you did, because everyone knows that only the finest dancers wind up in Nevada ... May I tell you a secret? I am most certain that if I were to inspect the city below, I would not discover a single person with more innate potential to become—with my training and guidance—a Broadway star. I know the idea may frighten you, and you may think about running away from it, but you are an entertainer, an artist. An artist! And inside you want nothing more than to shine like the jewel you are. Imagine entering the stage and the entire audience is waiting to observe your tiniest movement, waiting to experience—through you—the magic that allows them a rare encounter with the depths of their humanity. Think of what you could be, and all you have to do is say "yes." "Yes. I do have what it takes." "Yes, I am willing to do whatever I can to get there." "Yes—I am an artist, and like the sunrise follows the night, I must shine!" Unless you'd rather remain an unemployed tart with bad hair. I can see how difficult a choice that must be.

Changes

PAUL, a New York architect and self-proclaimed bachelor, convinces his fiancée why he should not change for her.

PAUL: Admit it. You fell in love with me thinking, he's great, all I have to do is change this, this, and this about him, and he'll be perfect. But I wouldn't be perfect, because every time I change for you, you take a tiny piece of my ... *(Gesturing to his testicles)* my you-know-whats. And one day, if I let you, you'd wake up next to a man with no you-know-whats. But then you'd have no use for me, so you'd find some other guy who still has his you-know-whats, because, in the end, what you and every woman really wants is a man who keeps a hold of his you-know-whats. And you can't help it. It's part of your nature. Look at Adam and Eve. After she eats the apple, she realizes that Adam isn't perfect for her anymore. So she goes up to him and says, "Here, eat this. Change for me or it will never work between us." And still being innocent, he says, "Sure. Anything for you sweetheart." And as she sliced that piece of apple, the first man's you-know-whats fell on the garden floor. And that is not cynicism; it's truth, and men have been struggling to keep a hold of their you-know-whats ever since ... Could you please point those scissors in the other direction?

No. 9

LEAPOLD, a composer, enlightens his wife to his distaste for the societal elite.

LEAPOLD: I thought I was invited to dinner, but Karl had invited me so I could play. I was infuriated. Of course, I played. I played like I had never played before, just me, and my keys. My music. I didn't even see them go off to dinner. The maid came and asked if I should want something. How could I have let myself believe they would accept me for anything more than a lackey? ... I never want to see them again, Josephine. I'd rather be thrown into the poor house and starve to death than be treated like a pet. That's what I am to them. That's what I've always been. A pretty little pet doing pretty little tricks for a precious little treat. Well, I don't need their patronage—It will never happen again. There are many princes and noblemen in this world. There is only one Leopold. Only one! Karl shall never hear my music again. I don't care what he's done for me. He is dead to me. Do you hear me? He is dead. I curse him and every note I played tonight. It is all cursed.

American Dixie

JODNER, a successful African American entertainer who has returned to the rural south to re-connect with his past, confronts a red neck in a local bar.

JODNER: *(Speaking In an affected Anglo dialect.)* I'm usually a peaceful man, but if you wish to confront me intelligibly, I propose you lift your derriere off that stool and make your way over here, *(Speaking in street dialect)* you garrulous, red-necked, tattoo-wearing, tobacco-chewing, confederate flag-waving angel. I bet the ladies think you are quite the catch—with your good old boy charm, your eighth grade education, and your five—sorry—four teeth. *(Speaking in Standard British dialect.)* But I'll extricate your central incisors, and I'll place them down your thoracic cavity so fast and so far that you'll be whistling Dixie out the other end on your next exhalation. *(Jodner hums the tune, "Away down south in Dixie," as he pulls up his shirtsleeves. Speaking in street dialect.)* What you don't know, "boy," is I love my south. And it's time we rid ourselves of the ignorant fools giving our land a bad name. This is my home, my country, and if you don't want to respect that— "in Dixie Land I'll make my stand, to live and die in Dixie." *(Gestures for stranger to get up off his chair and eight white males stand up to face him. Speaking in Standard British dialect.)* Perhaps I was unclear. I didn't mean all of you. I was addressing this good-looking chap here—unless of course you'd all rather dance.

Lexicons

HENRY, a computer analyst who was recently fired from his job and divorced by his wife, begs his brother for help.

HENRY: So I say, "You think I'm difficult to understand? I have a tri-syllabic friend who has difficulty ordering coffee!" *(Laughs hard and loud. His laughter turns into tears of pain.)* She left me Freddy. She's gone. She told me I was too esoteric for her. Esoteric? I am a plethora of amalgamated personifications, but I am not esoteric! What am I? The Tantra? She can't live with my preciosities. So I proceed with an attempt to elucidate a promise to ameliorate, and she simply laughs in my face and calls me precocious. I express that her connoting was fatuous—My preciosities ... She detests my meticulousness—I'm persnickety, Freddy, I'm persnickety! Have you understood anything I've said, or has it all been a dialectical exposition of nonsensical sounds to you? Are there any homo sapiens alive homologous with my level of verbal communication? Is there anyone here who could bestow upon us the meaning, connotation, or denotation of the word incertitude?   Otiose? *Aphasia?!* *(Beat.)* I'm sorry. I know I haven't seen you in a very long time, Freddy, but I am your brother. Help me ... help me, Freddy. Please.

Stichometry

JORGEN, an Education Lobbyist, rebukes a powerful senator for not supporting an increase in grants.

JORGEN: Yes, I understand your position, Senator. Thank you for taking the time to talk with—at—me, and—no, please don't get up, Sir. I can find my own way out. But before I go, I would like to ask you one last question. What did you mean when you said, "The best laid plans of mice and men"? Do you really believe lower-income students receiving grants will be unable to gain financial independence with an education, or they are too ignorant to learn? Or—are you talking about a pack of mice sitting in a field somewhere debating Hegel and Nietzsche and planning our demise until the inevitable farm plow upturns their nest? It must be the mice, because I'm sure that even you, Sir, with your tired eyes, pickled kidney, and triple bypasses would never want to squelch a program that could help keep this nation strong well into the future, simply because you didn't see any political gain in it for you. Let me be forthright, Senator. I will make certain your constituents know your position on the issue, and I will continue to fight for funding until either the masses rise to silence you, or your little nest here is upturned. Because you may hold me off, you may even put a bullet in the back of my head, but this mouse is only one of many mice and our best-laid plans are not shattered dreams along a California creek. Enjoy your lunch, Sir, and have one for me.

Contact

MACON, frightened he may become a ward of the state, tries desperately to get his older brother's attention.

MACON: I know we both need time to sort things out, but you're not even trying. Look at you. That bottle's eaten so much of you there's nothing left. You're nothing more than a jaded shard of dull glass hanging from a dead tree. I wrote that about you in Samuelson's class yesterday. Do you like it? I read it out loud in front of everyone, and I told them it was about you. Did you hear me?! ... *Did you hear me?* (Silence.) I'm not ready for another funeral, Donny. Mom and Dad are gone—but not everybody is dead. Have you thought about that? We didn't all die that day. Some of us are still living with it, and maybe we need you to live it with us. I can't do it alone. You're all I have left, and *(Fighting back the tears)* I need you here, Donny ... I need you.

Finding Forensics

CAL, a pizza deliveryman with dreams of becoming a film star, tries to convince his date to watch him make love to the camera.

CAL: I have to tell you a little secret ... In my bedroom, I have a video camera and a tripod that has clothes on it. It's nothing odd or anything, just a sequin dress, a shoulder length wig, and some sparkly red pumps. And before we watch the movie, I have to make love to it—the camera that is. You can watch if you'd like. I would love it if you'd watch. I have stuffed animals in director's chairs, but I'm comfortable with Tickle Me and Potty With Elmo watching, so you could— No, no, please. I want to be a film star, and I'm terribly frightened of people watching, and I have this aversion to glass—well, lenses actually—so every night *(She walks away.)* ... All right then, go. Go! Go ahead and leave. But when I make it big, I'll be telling this story to that pretentious guy on "Inside the Actors Studio." And when he asks me what I hate, it will be you! It will be the sound of you! And when he asks me what I hope God will say when I die. It will be, "Don't worry, Alyssa's not here. She didn't make it because she left you and Tickle and Potty in your greatest moment of need!" ... It was the red pumps. I knew I shouldn't have bought those sparkly red pumps.

Changes

PAUL, a New York architect and former self-proclaimed bachelor, tries to convince his fiancée that he must be free to laugh how he wants.

PAUL: No, no, you said, "Do you have to laugh?" You didn't say, "Could you laugh a little softer?" And it was a very funny movie. You saw me rocking in my chair trying not to laugh, and you didn't say anything. I nearly killed myself from holding it in, but you didn't say a thing. And at some point in there, it became very clear to me that you'd never heard the story of the ancient funny people—No, you have to listen to this; it's crucial that you listen to this. Because a long, long, long time ago—very long ago—there was this tribe that prayed to the God of laughter. Now, they were a small tribe, but they had a lot of funny people. And one day, some of the unfunny tribes came into their territory and found the funny people to be different. So they tried to change them. But the funny people wouldn't stop laughing. So they enslaved them, and tortured them, took their homes, their land—they even killed them, but they couldn't stop the funny people from laughing. So they tried to exterminate them. Tried to wipe out the funny people—and my point is, I'm the only survivor. I'm it, the last of the funny people. With me a whole race may die. So my laughter can't be held back. It must reach to the sky and be free to express itself. The last funny person must laugh! But not so loud. A little softer. I understand. Soft enough to not upset the unfunny people—I get it. And you'll let me know how loud that is next time, right, oh Grand Poobah of laughter?

Chanuka

MUNNY, a highly intelligent stoner attending an elite university, informs his professor why he shouldn't be penalized for his lack of attendance.

MUNNY: You heard me wrong, Professor. Like you, I want to be a part of the east coast intelligential line of hyperbole-attic elitist-ical superior, but you see, my genome fields reject the idea of the worker bee syndrome and only hear the iconoclastic philosophical ality of Bo Jungle ness and the rhythm of life. People dance and people die. I chose to dance—albeit, not very well—but if I lose a letter grade because of class attendance, then I'll be forced to turn on the proactive post-procrastinate-a-tive burners and purchase two tickets to paradise because what you fail to vision-ate in your pataphysical phylogenetic state, is that I, Munny Mars, pay your wage, have a ninety-eight percent in your class, and could well be the anti-Christ. Yes, that is correct, Sir. Teleolological studies are revelatory—September 11th, ecocide, the Red Sox—"When towers tumble and the Bambino's curse is lifted, woe to he that still liv-es-ith." The book of Marsicle, verse 66. Read it. Live it. Be it. And if I am, indeed, he-she-it-or other—which I have a pretty good idea I am, in concurrence with the magic ball of eight, and this little girl down the street in a yellow dress—I could make it problematical when I inhale my supremacy-ness's, and therefore, a re-cognate-tiation of your ardencies relating to attendance policies should be aborted immediately, or at least re-visionate-ed for those of us who will one day have superpowers. *(Beat.)* No Sir, the deity is not above doing multiple extra credit assignments.

Ursa Minor

MELVIN, a cab driver, informs his friend that his honeymoon days are over.

MELVIN: It's over Moe. The honeymoon is over. Ninety-two days, seventeen hours, thirty-three minutes, and it's gone. I guess some guys wouldn't ask for more than that, but I was, Moe, I was. Call me crazy for thinking it could last forever, but don't call me a honeymooner because those days are ancient history. Every Saturday it was a hot shower and nice cologne for me, some sexy underwear for her, and edible lotions, and little love notes—but not any more, Moe, not any more. You want to know what I got on Saturday to celebrate my birthday? A one hundred and twenty-nine piece all-purpose ratchet set. A ratchet set, Moe. Period. No love note, no underwear, no lotions, nothing—'cause she's tired and has a headache, on a Saturday, on my birthday! You know what this means, don't you? It means I'm already living in the garage, and she's sitting in the house reading cheap romance novels with legs she hasn't shaved for a year. And all for what, Moe, ninety-two days, seventeen hours, and thirty-three minutes? I'm going to ask her for a re-run. I'm going to demand a re-run, or a sequel, or a do- over, or something... Do I look fat to you?

The Phoenician Prince

TOM, a proud carrier of the Unites States mail, defends his honor.

TOM: I know you think I'm an ignorant hick, but I'm smart enough to understand your double entendres, and see the exchange of looks between you and your colleague when I enter the room. You must wonder what my wife—a scholar of such promise—could ever see in a man like me. I must have other assets. That could be the only reason, right Doctor? Well, I may not speak your lexicon, but I'm not the picaro you think I am. I'm a United States postal carrier, and every day I bring joy into a world that you will never see. I deliver letters to an African-American mother of two from her husband in upstate New York, and each letter brings her words of hope to go on waiting. I deliver letters from Indonesia to a husband who is lonesome for his wife and children, and each letter takes a little of his heartache away. I deliver mail to senior citizens who look forward to my arrival every day, because they don't have much else to look forward to. And I get to see their faces light up when they receive a letter from a loved one, which they'll tell me about for weeks to come, and I count myself privileged that they would share the happiness they desperately need with me ... If you would be so kind as to excuse my expeditious, extemporaneous expostulating, I'll be extricating my extraneousness for the evening. Good night, Sir, and please, enjoy your dinner.

When Love Comes Along

STYLES, an uptight and fast-talking intellectual, informs his indecisive girlfriend that it's impossible for him to know what she wants before she knows it.

STYLES: What do you want from me? I'd give you my heart, and my kidneys, and every fiber of my effervescent being, but I can't give you what I don't have. I'm not you! I can't give you—you! That's what you're asking for, isn't it? For me to know what you know before you even know that you know, so when you know, I'll already know before you're knowing what you'll know. I can't know that! That I know. Right now, I think I want the shrimp bisque with a side of pumpernickel. Did you know that before I knew that I knew that? No. So the real question is, can you be happy with me not knowing? People are waiting, Cupcake. Either you decide now or we just won't eat, because I don't think I should partake if you don't, even if you think I should—in case you were thinking I should. And if you were thinking I should, it was merely coincidence that I knew. I didn't actually know before you knew, which is the issue, isn't it? And the kind of soup you want, that I need to know as well? So let me know when you know, because I don't know. I knew it was going to be like this. Oh, I knew. I knew before you knew that you wouldn't know, that, I know I knew! I'll have the Yellow Pepper soup with Serrano Cream. *(Beat.)* Ah, make that two.

Traversing Transudation

MARTY, a political science major, persuades his date that he does his part to be eco-friendly.

MARTY: Stop right there! I know who you're talking about, OK? But I realize the quantitative restraints on the world's environment and the tragic consequences. I realize the need for new forms of thinking that would lead to a fundamental revision of human behavior. I, too, am convinced that a rapid redressing of the present unbalanced and dangerously deteriorating world situation is the primary task facing humanity, but styrofoam was all they had, and I was very hungry. And I know they support—but one salad is not going to—OK, one burger and a salad is not—OK, two burgers, a salad, fries and a sliver of pie—is not going to kill the rain forest vital to man's existence. And the tank of gas? That company doesn't drill in the gulf anymore; that's over—right? So that doesn't count. And sure, I take long showers and toss a good amount of plastic out, but I do what I can—Oh, I always carry a condom, so I do my part to defuse the population explosion. That should count for something, right? *(She walks away.)* That's not fair. You told me you were religious about being green. How was I supposed to know you were Catholic?

Optative Dep

JOHNATHAN, a famous film director, explains why he couldn't return home to watch his father die.

JOHNATHAN: Don't start Pat, please. I know I only have two more minutes, but I'm having a little problem. I can hear him talking, and you know what he's saying? He's saying, "Who the hell are all these people, and what the hell are they doing here?" He's saying, "Where were you? A man is dying of cancer for six months and you don't come to see him? On his deathbed for nearly two weeks and still you don't come?" And the thing is, I couldn't. I loved him so much that I couldn't watch him die. *(On the verge of tears.)* And he was waiting for me, Pat. He was waiting ... I'm sorry. I'm so sorry, Pops ... If you want me to say something, it's going to be what he wants me to say: "Jesus, Mary and Joseph, what some people won't do for Shepard's Pie and some good Protestant whiskey." You'd like that, wouldn't you, Pops? *(He laughs. His laughter turns to tears. Beat.)* Maybe you should do the eulogy.

Awares

RON, a young science teacher, informs his future wife why he feels it imperative they leave her sister's house.

RON: I'm just requesting—strongly that we get a hotel room for the last few days of your conference. It's a long drive for you, and we could have a little more time together. It's not that I don't like your sister. She's great to let us stay here and everything, but it's like working out at the gym for seven and a half hours just to have a conversation with her. "Are you going to make it back for the wedding, Sarah?" *(As Sarah.)* "This is a conch shell." Oh, O.K. Can you say lithium drip? I never believed in aliens messing with people's minds, but she makes a good case for the possibility. "You certainly have nice weather this time of year, Sarah." *(As Sarah.)* "Caribbean Lobster tail and Bridgewater Toffee can be nice." Oh, O.K. O.K., great and powerful mistress of the non sequitur. I know she's your sister, but it's creepy, sweetie. Do you think maybe Randall drugs her? Keeps his own little Stepford wife doped up and at peace in a world all her own? I'm serious. It's like "Night of the Living Dead," "Dawn of the Dead," and "Zombies Revenge" all rolled up in one out here. I swear, if I chopped off her arm, dust would fall out of her empty limb, all the other zombie wives would converge upon the house, and when you returned, I would be one of them. Is that what you want?

Performance Rights

Monologue Writing Opportunity

One of the key objectives for this book is to encourage writers to start writing active monologues so actors and teachers have access to appropriate pieces for auditions and class work. To this end, I seek talented writers to submit two of their best active monologues for an opportunity to have their work published in a future volume of *Active Monologues That Directors Want to Hear.*

Monologue entries must adhere to the following guidelines:
1) Monologues should be 45-120 seconds in length
2) A majority of the dialogue should use active form
3) Be addressed to one partner in the present moment
4) Allow listener to grasp character relationships and basic argument of the event early in the piece
5) Adhere to rules of decency
6) Include title of play or monologue, character name, brief description of character speaking and their relationship to invisible partner and event
7) Entries must be original and applicant must be owner and controller of copyright
8) Submission is restricted to monologues that have not been previously published

Writers will retain all rights to their monologue material.

For a complete list of guidelines and submission information go to: ACTIVEMONOLOGUES.COM

About the Author

Paul D. Bawek is an award winning actor, director, playwright, fight choreographer, and acting coach. He's taught acting for the stage and screen, playwriting, and directing at theatres and educational institutions across the nation and abroad. Published works include *Mithridatism* (Playwrights' Center Monologues for Women), *Changes*, *FirstKiss*, and *The Director as Storyteller*. Produced works include *CrossRoads, Falsies, The Cabin, Changes, First Kiss*, and *No Fault*. Paul also co-authored the scripts for *Jack London Tales, Gold Country Tales*, and *Twain Tales*, which played at schools throughout Northern California. As an actor, Paul worked at the B Street Theatre where he co-starred with Timothy Busfield in the world premiere of Aaron Sorkin's full-length version of *Hidden in This Picture*. He also performed at The Studio Theatre, The Fantasy Theatre, Santa Rosa Repertory Theatre, and the Bloomsbury Theatre in London, UK. He was the commercial spokesperson for The Bank of Stockton, United Interstate Financial, Port of Subs, and a reporter/interviewer of the Oakland A's baseball players for KSCH TV in Northern California. Paul's professional and academic directing credits include the world premiere of the British comedy *Average* at the Bolivar Theatre in London, UK, and *CrossRoads* at the Studio Theatre in Sacramento, CA. Other directing credits include work at The B Street/Fantasy Theatre, The Magic Circle Repertory, American River College, and Southwest Minnesota State University, where two of his productions received the Kennedy Center American College Theatre Festival Award for best ensemble acting. Mr. Bawek is currently the head of the B.F.A. acting program at Florida Southern College.

Notes

Notes

Notes